Micro Ran

- !

Constable Country Walks

15 Circular Walks in and around the Stour Valley, including
Flatford Mill, Dedham, Polstead and Nayland

Geoff Gostling

ISBN 0-9525478-4-8

Printed by Portman Press
Published by G J Gostling
Copyright © G J Gostling

Cover Picture: Flatford Mill

CONTENTS

Foreword   3

Introduction   4

About the Area   4

Walks

Foreword

Micro Ramblers are local walk books.   Each book in the series contains 15 walks in a comparatively small area. These are almost always circular, and often linked so that two or more may be joined to form longer walks if required.

Instructions for each individual walk are contained on the right-hand page, with the relevant map on the left, so there's no need to turn over pages while you're walking (unless you're joining 2 or more together).

The average length of walks in this book is 6½km (4 miles). The scale of sketch maps is 4cm to 1km or 2½in to 1 mile. (Not the overall map on page 36)

All walks use rights of way*, permissive paths or unclassified roads. Limited use is made of main roads for joining paths or getting to and from car parks.

Distances are given in metres and kilometres. If you're more at home with yards and miles, it may be of help to remember that 1 yard is about 1 metre, 800 metres is a half-mile, 1½km is about 1 mile.

Times are based on average walking speeds. As a rough guide, at an average walking speed, it takes about 12 minutes to walk 1km, or just over 1 minute to walk 100m.

Country Walking

Right of Way means that you have a right of passage over the ground, but no right to stray from the path.   You also have a right to expect that paths be unobstructed. Clearly farmers have to work the land, but footpaths should be rolled within 2 weeks of ploughing, if weather permits.

Please remember the Country Code.   Machinery, livestock and crops are the farmers livelihood.   Help them, and help preserve wildlife by observing a few simple rules:

Guard against risk of fire;	Take litter home
Protect wildlife plants & trees;	Use gates & stiles to cross fences;
Fasten gates;	Leave livestock alone;
Keep pets under control;	Don't pollute water;
Keep to rights of way;	Don't make unnecessary noise;

Introduction

John Constable was born in East Bergholt in 1776. To our good fortune, he resisted following his father into the family milling business, and concentrated on his painting instead.

The term 'Constable Country' first came into use in his lifetime, and survived since then. It describes the area in and around the Stour Valley that he loved and painted.

Using this book, you can explore various villages and surrounding footpaths in Constable Country. Complete all of the walks and you'll know most of the Stour valley from Cattawade (Brantham) to Nayland.

Whilst the walk instructions are meant to be self-contained, you may find Landranger maps 155 and 168 useful in getting to start points.

There's a long distance trail called the Stour Valley Path, which extends from Newmarket to Cattawade. This was laid out by the Dedham Vale and Stour Valley Countryside Project, whose aims are to improve access to the countryside. Details of the trail and other walks in the area are available from their department at the County Council offices in Ipswich.

For walks in this book, frequent use has been made of sections of the Stour Valley path, and another long distance path called the Essex Way. For this reason, you'll often be told to follow 'Stour Valley Path' or 'Essex Way' signs. Pay careful attention to the instructions so that you don't follow these signs too far - you could end up in Newmarket or Epping!

Several diversion applications are outstanding in the Stoke-by-Nayland area. It's not clear if these will be accepted, so it's been impossible to give instructions to this effect. Therefore, if the instructions in the book disagree with waymarks on the ground, please observe the waymarks.

About the Area

Cattawade: This is the first crossing place on the Stour. It's probably best known for the plastics factory, built around the turn of the century. There's one pub in the village - the Crown.

Dedham: Dedham church featured in many of Constable's paintings. (it didn't matter what he was painting at the time!) The village is popular, and gets crowded at weekends. Refreshments are available at Essex Rose café, the Dedham Centre restaurant, Marlborough Head, and Sun Hotel.

East Bergholt: Birthplace of John Constable. St. Mary's church is interesting, not least because of the upside-down bells in the churchyard.

Flatford Mill: One of the mills owned by John Constable's father. It stands next to Willy Lott's cottage, pictured in the 'Haywain'. They are both owned by the National Trust, and are a location for courses run by the Field Studies Council.

Higham: Another village well known to Constable. Well known by name too, by passers-by on the nearby A12, for the Higham point-to-point races. There used to be a pub in the village, but it's now a private house.

Langham: The church and hall stand alone above the Stour Valley, well apart from the rest of the village. No refreshments here either I'm afraid!

Nayland: An attractive village on the Essex Suffolk border, as far as this book takes us. There's an original Constable in St James Church. 1 pub, the Anchor Inn; a restaurant, the White Hart, and the Mill Stores café.

Polstead: A pleasant little village, made notorious by Maria Marten, victim of the Red Barn Murder. There's 1 pub, the Cock Inn .

Stoke-by-Nayland: The church of St Mary was one of Constable's favourites. Standing 120' (36m) tall, in a village that stands on a hill, it's the most prominent feature for miles around. There are 3 pubs/inns. The Angel Inn, the Black Horse and the Crown.

Stratford St Mary: This used to be on the main London road, but thankfully has now been bypassed. There are some interesting old buildings along the main street, with some unfortunate modern insertions. There are 3 pubs, The Anchor, The Swan and the Black Horse.

Thorington Street: A small village with some attractive buildings on the B1068 between Higham and Stoke-by-Nayland. There's 1 pub, the Rose Inn. (This is highly popular at weekends, and it's wise to book)

Map 1

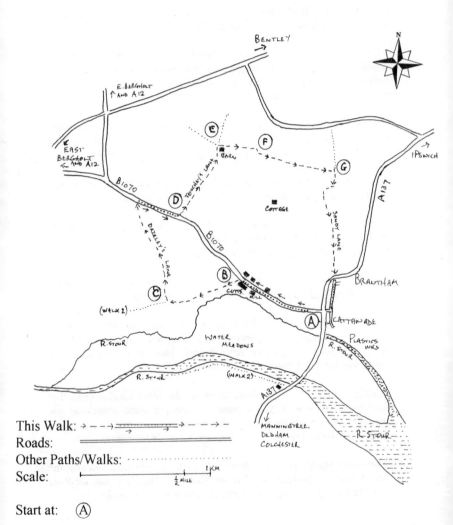

This Walk: → – – → ⟹ → – – → –
Roads: ═══════
Other Paths/Walks: ⋯⋯⋯⋯⋯
Scale: |—————————————————| 1 KM
                    ½ MILE

Start at: Ⓐ

Walk 1

Distance: 5½km (3½m) 1-1½ hours
Start Point: Cattawade (Brantham) (GR 101332)
Route: Dazeley's Lane, Touchey's Lane, Sandy Lane
Pubs: The Crown, Cattawade
Car Park: Cattawade picnic site, off B1070 near T-junction with A137

A: Go onto the B1070 and turn left. In about 550m you'll pass Brantham
Mill, and about 100m further you'll pass some cottages on the left.

B: After the last of the cottages, turn left on a signposted field edge path.
This soon becomes a narrow lane, and in about 200m you'll reach a stile
into open fields. Cross the stile, and continue for another 200m to reach a
stile and a gate into Dazeley's lane on the right hand side.

C: Cross the stile and walk up the lane. At the top, turn right on the road
(B1070) for about 350m to reach a gateway into another lane on the left.

D: Turn left into the lane (Touchey's Lane).   Stay on this pleasant path,
following the edge of a wood for about 500m. When the lane leaves the
wood, keep on in more or less the same direction to reach an old barn.

E: Pass immediately left of the barn to find a 4-way FP sign. Here turn
right, then, just after the barn, turn left into a gap in the field, then
immediately right along the field edge. You should now have turned right
from your original course, along a field edge with a hedge on your right.
*(Passing to the right of the barn and through the gap in the hedge would
achieve the same object, but it isn't a right of way!).*

F: Follow the field edge for 300m to reach a good track on a corner.
Here go right and left to keep more or less straight on. In about 150m,
where a track goes right towards an isolated cottage, again keep straight
on. In about another 500m, you'll reach a good track at a T-junction.

G: Turn right at the T-junction and stay on this track (Sandy Lane) to
reach Cattawade. At the road, cross over and go straight down Cattawade
Street. When you reach the Crown at the bottom turn right to cross the
A137 and return to the picnic site through a gate way.

Map 2

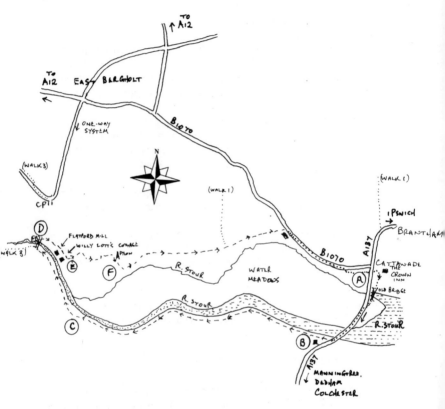

This Walk: → - - → → ──→ → → - - → →
Roads: ═══════════════
Other Paths/Walks: · · · · · · · · · · · · · ·
Scale: |——————————| 1 KM
                      ½ MILE

Start at: (A)

Walk 2

Distance: 7km (4½m) 1½-2 hours
Start Point: Cattawade (Brantham) (GR 101332)
Route: Stour, Flatford Mill, Willy Lott's Cottage
Pubs: The Crown, Cattawade
Car Park: Cattawade picnic site, off B1070 near T-junction with A137

A: Go out onto the picnic site access road, and turn right to cross the main A137. On the other side take the path down onto the old road, and walk along to the Crown. Turn right at the Crown to cross the old road bridge, and continue on to reach the footway along the A137. Walk along to cross the next bridge in about 300m.

B: After crossing the bridge, take the signed footpath to the right along the river embankment. In about 2km, after passing under power lines, keep right where the embankment forks, crossing 2 stiles almost immediately. Keep on to reach a stile by the N.T. sign for Lower Barn Farm.

C: Cross the stile and turn right alongside the concrete dam.   Continue along the well-surfaced track on the other side, soon passing Flatford Mill, and Flatford Lock. Cross the river when you reach the footbridge.

D: Turn right along the narrow road on the other side, passing the tearoom. Stay on the road as far as the gate into the Field Centre car park, next to Willy Lott's cottage.

E: When you reach Willy Lott's cottage, turn left on a signed footpath. After a right and left turn on this well trodden lane, continue for about another 150m, to find a footpath sign taking you into the field on the left. *(The lane continues as the Flatford circular walk).* Continue along in the same direction on the other side of the hedge to the pylon, then turn right along the field edge to reach a stile in the next corner.

F: After crossing the stile turn left and keep on in more or less the same direction to reach the B1070 near Brantham Mills. *If in doubt, follow the Stour Valley walk signs - they take you back to your start point.* At the B1070, turn right and follow the road back to the picnic site.

Map 3

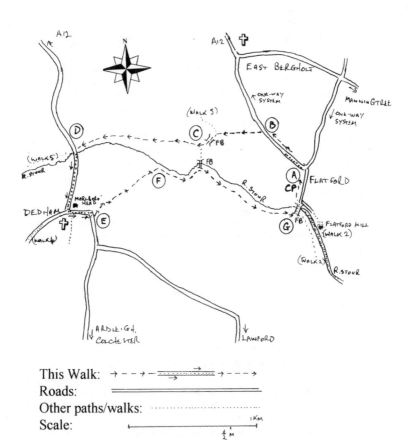

This Walk: → - - → — ⇒ → - - →
Roads: ═══════════
Other paths/walks: ···················
Scale: |————————————| 1 Km
                        ½ M

Start at: Ⓐ

Walk 3

Distance: 6½km (4m) 1½-2 hours
Start Point: Flatford (GR 076336)
Route: Dedham and Flatford
Pubs: Marlborough Head and Sun Hotel (both at Dedham)
Car Park: Main car park, Flatford

A: From the car park, go out onto the road and turn left following the one-way system. In about 250m take the path on the right parallel to the road. Stay on the upper path for about 300m until the road bends right.

B: At the bend in the road, cross the wide metal stile into the field straight ahead, and follow the signed path down the hill. Cross a similar stile at the bottom of the field, and continue more or less straight on, almost immediately crossing a bridge over a side branch of the Stour.

C: Shortly after the bridge, fork right to continue along parallel to the main track for a short distance, soon turning right in a pleasant leafy lane. Keep straight on along the lane and at the end in about 400m go through a kissing gate to continue on the same line across the field. When you reach the river, keep on along the bank to reach a road.

D: At the road, turn left to reach a T-junction by the Marlborough Head in about 500m. Turn left at the T-junction, and walk along as far as the right hand bend.

E: On the bend, turn diagonally left on a signed path across the field following a wide track. *(The official right of way is to enter the field by a stile down the short drive on the left, just after the bend).* At the other side of the field, bear slightly right then left again on a clear signed path down to the river bank.

F: At the river turn right and follow it for about 2km to reach the footbridge at Flatford.

G: At Flatford, cross the bridge, turn left on the road, and in a few metres turn left up some steps and along a metalled path to return to the car park..

Map 4

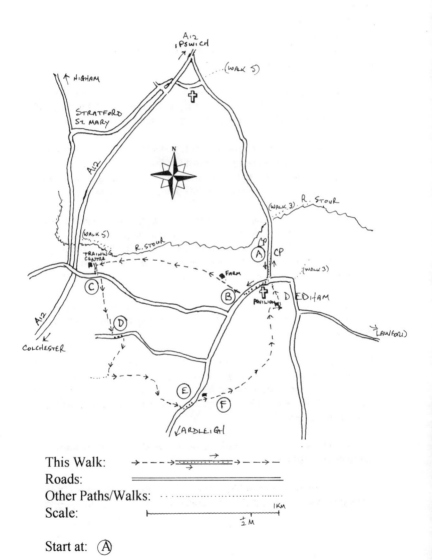

This Walk: →– – –→ ═══→═══ →– –→ –
Roads: ═══════════
Other Paths/Walks: ·······················
Scale: ├─────────────────┤ 1 Km
              ½ M

Start at: Ⓐ

Walk 4

Distance: 5½km (3½m) 1-1½ hours
Start Point: Dedham   (GR 057336)
Route: Essex Way and Dedham circular
Pubs: Marlborough Head and the Sun Hotel
Car Park: see parking for walk 5

A: Walk up the road from the car park into Dedham. Turn right at the junction passing the church, and walk along the road for 250m to reach a FP sign on the right (Essex way and circular walk 2).

B: Turn right on the Essex Way, passing a farm in about 250m. In another 400m go through a kissing gate on the right and continue in the same direction on the other side of the hedge. Follow 'circular walk 2' signs until you emerge on a side road opposite the Royal London Insurance residential training centre. Turn left here to reach the Stratford road.

C: At the Stratford road cross to the signed footpath almost opposite. From the stile go slightly left uphill to the left hand edge of a small wood near the top of the hill. Here cross another stile and continue uphill inside the fence alongside the wood. Stay on the same line to reach a road in about 300m.

D: Turn left at the road, and in about 150m turn right down Monks lane. At the bottom of the lane keep left and immediately after crossing a brook turn left and follow it to reach a road in about 700m.

E: Turn left at the road, and in about 50m ignore the signed 'No.2' path, and walk on a few steps to take a signed path to the right going past the front of Brook Farm House. Keep left of the 'Nissen hut' garage and leave the bottom of the garden through a metal gate *(note this is someone's garden, so do please close the gate).*

F: After leaving the garden, continue along the field edge, now following signs for Circular path No.1. Follow the ditch for about 600m to a stile, then follow 'No. 1' signs through meadows and parkland via kissing gates and stiles to reach the playing fields behind Dedham Church. Turn right to pass behind the pavilion then left back to Dedham village centre.

Map 5

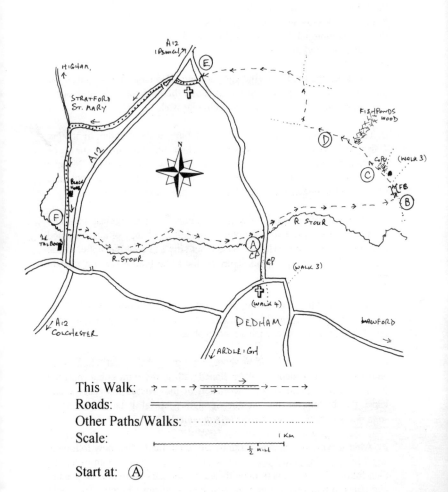

This Walk: → – – → ⇒⇒⇒ → – – →
Roads: ══════
Other Paths/Walks: ·················
Scale: ├─────────┤ 1 KM
                ½ MILE

Start at: Ⓐ

Walk 5

Distance: 8km (5m) 1½-2 hours
Start Point: Dedham   (GR 057336)
Route: Stratford St Mary Church and village
Pubs: The Anchor, The Swan and Black Horse
Car Park: Free riverside car park on B1029 between A12 and Dedham

A: Leave the riverside car park and turn left. Immediately after crossing the bridge over the river, take the signed footpath on the right and walk along the river bank. At a waymark sign in about 350m, leave the river bank at a slight angle to reach a kissing gate into a pleasant leafy lane. Follow the lane until it bends left and merges with a wider track.

B: Keep on in the same direction, crossing a metal railed plank bridge in about 75m, and a few steps further, turn left at the junction.   In about 100m, turn left over a stile and walk along the edge of the small wood for about 50m to cross another stile.

C: Walk along the field edge path with the fence on your left for about 200m. Cross the stile into the next field, this time with a hedge on your right. In about 100m cross a stile on the right, to continue once again with the fence on your left. After another stile you'll cross the end of a narrow wood (Fishponds Wood). When you reach the other side, turn right for a few steps, then turn left along a pleasant leafy lane.

D: The lane soon becomes a field edge path. In a further 100m, turn right uphill on a signed lane. At the top of the hill, at a 4-way sign, turn left to follow a good track, taking you roughly in the direction of Stratford St Mary church. About 75m before the main track bends sharp left, cross a plank bridge to the right and continue parallel to the track. Where the track bends left, go straight on across the field to the gap on the other side.

E: At the road on the other side, turn left, then turn right to pass the church. Pass under the A12, follow the road round to the left, and stay on it all the way through Stratford St Mary village (about 1½km).

F: About 350m after passing the Black Horse, and about 100m before reaching 'Le Talbooth' restaurant, turn left under a wide tunnel under the A12 and follow the river bank all the way back to your start point.

Map 6

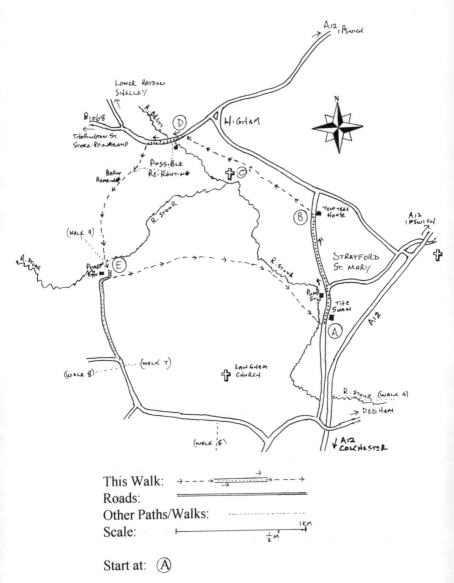

This Walk:
Roads:
Other Paths/Walks:
Scale: 1 KM ½ M

Start at: Ⓐ

Walk 6

Distance: 6km (3½m) 1-1½ hours
Start Point: Stratford St Mary (GR 043342)
Route: Higham and Stratford St Mary
Pubs: The Swan, Stratford St Mary
Car Park: Roadside parking near the Swan

A: Walk along the main road with the Swan on your right. Where the main road bends right, continue straight on along the narrower road.

B: In about 500m, soon after passing open fields on the right, turn left onto a farm track opposite the gates to Yew Tree House. You'll soon be walking along the field edge, with a wire fence on your left. Keep on towards the farm buildings at the far end of the field. *(At the time of writing, the right of way is a direct line along the field towards the right hand edge of the buildings, but local usage favours following the field edge down the field, then turning right to pass the buildings, to reach the same point.)* If the definitive path is signed or rolled, use it, otherwise keep to the field edge.

C: At the corner of the buildings, enter the wooden railed paddock via the stile on the corner. Walk along with the rail on your left to reach a stile in the next corner. Cross the church drive, go through a metal kissing gate, and cross 2 fields to reach the road in Lower Street, Higham.

D: Turn left on the road to cross the River Brett. In 250m* turn left on a signed path to cross the field. (*NB At time of writing, there's an application to divert the path round 2 field edges, shortly after crossing the Brett. Use the field edge route if signs are in place and follow the path round to reach the same point.)* On the other side, cross the end of a lane and go through the gap opposite, passing along a field edge with a ditch on your left. In 150m, by some brick ruins, cross a stile and continue with the field edge on your right. In the next corner cross the stile and go straight on across the field towards a pump house. Cross 2 bridges to reach the road, and walk up to the bend.

E: Where the road bends right, turn left on the signed path across the field towards a gap in the hedge. At the next field edge, aim 50m right of the large house, and continue on, following yellow arrows to reach the bank of the Stour in about 500m. In another 200m, cross a stile into a large meadow and follow arrows half right to a stile on the far side. Cross the bridge to emerge on the main road in Stratford St Mary, then turn left to return to your car.

Map 7

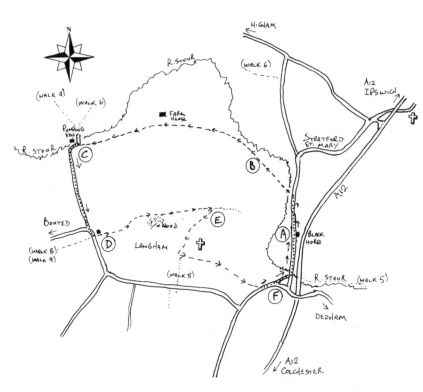

This Walk: → – – – → → ⋯⋯⋯⋯⋯⋯⋯ → → – – – →
Roads: ══════════════════════
Other Paths/Walks: ⋯⋯⋯⋯⋯⋯⋯⋯⋯⋯⋯⋯⋯⋯
Scale: |——————————————| 1 KM
                    ⊢—⊣ 1/2 MILE

Start at: Ⓐ

Walk 7

Distance: 6km (3½m) 1-1½ hours
Start Point: Stratford St Mary   (GR 042338)
Route: Stour Valley Path and the Essex Way
Pubs: Black Horse, Stratford St Mary
Car Park: Roadside parking near the Black Horse

A: Walk along the main road from the Black Horse with the pub on your right.   In about 300m turn left on a signed path taking you across the river by a concrete footbridge.   Cross the stile on the other side, and take the signed path diagonally to the far right hand corner of the field.

B: In the far corner cross a stile and follow the river bank.   In about 200m, go through a signposted gap on your left to continue in the same direction on the other side of the ditch. Keep more or less straight on, following signs for the Stour Valley path.   You'll soon pass a large farmhouse to your right. Follow the signs taking you onward across 2 more fields, emerging on a road at a corner near a large pump house.

C: Now leaving the Stour Valley path, stay on the road and follow it round to the left in about 50m. At the junction with another road in 600m go straight on for about 50m to reach a signposted track on the left.

D: Turn left on this wide track signed as the Essex Way.   In about 400m, keep left at the fork, then, just after the bend, cross a stile, a plank bridge and another stile into the field on the right. Follow the direction of the Essex Way sign taking you to a stile on the corner of a small wood. Continue on in more or less the same direction for about 500m to reach a signed track to your right.

E: Turn right and follow this good track uphill, to reach Langham Church in about 400m. About 100m after passing the church, by the gates of Langham Hall, turn left. Follow this private road for about 800m to reach the road at Gun Hill.

F: Turn left on the road, then go down the cul-de-sac to cut the corner and emerge by Le Talbooth restaurant. Turn left here, and follow the road back to your car in about 500m.

Map 8

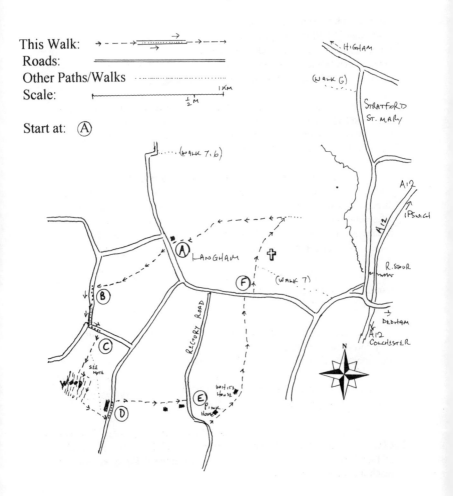

This Walk:

Roads:

Other Paths/Walks

Scale: 1 KM

½ M

Start at: Ⓐ

(WALK 7,6)

Ⓐ LANGHAM

Ⓑ

Ⓒ

SEE NOTE

Ⓓ

Ⓔ WHITE HOUSE

PINK HOUSE

RECTORY ROAD

Ⓕ (WALK 7)

HIGHAM

(WALK G)

STRATFORD ST. MARY

A12

A12

IPSWICH

R. STOUR

DEDHAM

A12 COLCHESTER

N

Walk 8

Distance: 6km (3½m) 1-1½ hours
Start Point: Langham (GR 027337)
Route: Essex Way and Langham Church
Pubs: Black Horse, Stratford St Mary is the nearest
Car Park: Roadside parking only *Go south through Stratford St Mary to top of Gun Hill. Turn right on road signed ·Langham. In ¾ mile (1200m) turn right down side road where main road bends left. Park in small unofficial lay-by 50m down on the left hand side or wide verge on right further down..*

A: Walk down the road and turn left across the field on the Essex Way. Follow signs to reach a narrow road in about 800m.

B: Turn left on the road, and walk up to the top. Turn left at the T-junction and walk along to the signed path on the right in about 100m.

C: Turn right on the path along the field edge. *The official right of way leaves the field edge diagonally in about 200m, but the following signed unofficial diversion is easier:* Keep straight on to the patch of sparse woodland in about 400m. Turn left along the woodland fence, and follow it round the next corner. At the 2nd corner turn left, away from the wood, to reach a stile onto a road in the corner by another wood on your right.

D: At the road turn left uphill for about 100m, then turn right on a signed track. In 500m follow the track left briefly, then cross a stile to go on in the same direction as before. In 200m you'll reach a road.

E: Turn right on the road for about 300m. At the bottom of the hill turn left on a signed track. After passing a pink timbered house on the left, keep straight on for about 250m, then, immediately after the drive to a white house on the left, follow the track round to the left to reach the road in 800m.

F: At the road, turn briefly right, then left again down the private road towards Langham Church. Go past the gates to Langham Hall, then keep on past the church, and down the hill. At the bottom, where the track passes through the hedge, turn left on a signed path In about 400m cross a stile, then go very slightly left to reach another 2 stiles into a lane. Turn left in the lane and walk along for about 400m to reach your start point.

Map 9

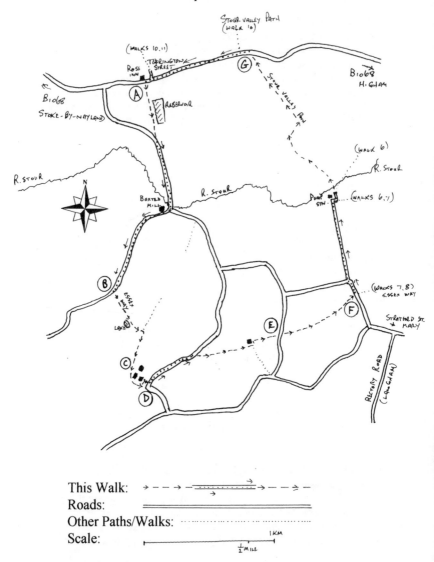

This Walk: → – → ↠ ⋯→ → → – → –
Roads: ═══════════
Other Paths/Walks: ⋯⋯⋯⋯⋯⋯⋯⋯
Scale: |——————————| 1 KM
                 |—½ MILE—|

Start at: Ⓐ

Walk 9

Distance: 8km (5m) 1½-2 hrs
Start Point: Thorington Street (GR 011353)
Route: Essex Way and Stour Valley Path
Pubs: The Rose, Thorington Street
Car Park: Small lay-by next to 'phone box in Thorington Street.

A: Go down the signed path opposite the Rose car park. Keep straight on past the reservoir to reach a narrow road in 500m. Turn left on the road and walk along to reach the hump-backed bridge by Boxted Mill. Keep right after the bridge, and stay on the road for about 800m to reach a signed track on the left hand side just after the wood at the top of the hill.

B: Turn left on the track (Essex Way). In about 400m, after passing a lake on the right, stay on the track as it climbs and bends to left then right.

C: Soon after passing a cottage on the left, just before farm buildings, turn right on a signed path.. At the next corner, turn left (again signed) following the field edge, and keep straight on for about 100m to reach another Essex Way sign taking you left behind an open barn. *In effect you should now have walked 3 sides of a rectangle round the edge of the farm buildings.* At the corner by the private road, turn right along the field edge to a double FP sign and exit the field onto the public road.

D: Go left on the road. In 500m, take the Essex Way across the field to the right. *(If in doubt, follow direction of sign)* Soon after joining a field edge at a corner, you'll pass a house. Shortly after this, go through the gap and continue on the track on the other side to reach a road in 200m.

E: At the road go briefly left then right again on the Essex Way to reach another road in 800m. This is where you leave the Essex Way.

F: At the road turn left, and at the corner in 50m go straight on along the narrow road. At the bottom, follow the road right past the pump house, then left. Cross 2 bridges, and follow the field edge on the left, signed the Stour Valley Path. In about 100m you'll join a clear track. Stay on this to reach the B1068. *(Don't miss the signed left hand turn in about 500m).*

G: When you reach the B1068, turn left and walk back *with great care* to Thorington Street.

Map 10

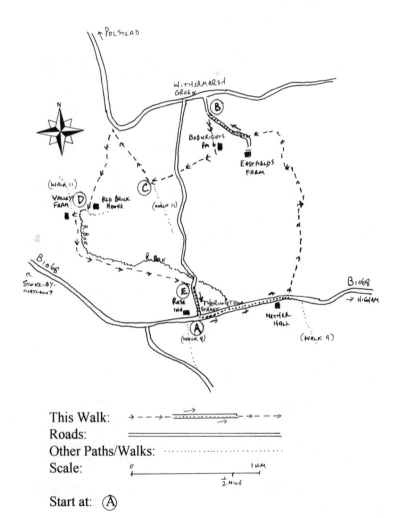

This Walk: → – → – → ▭→ → →– → →
Roads: ═══════════
Other Paths/Walks: ⋯⋯⋯⋯⋯⋯⋯⋯
Scale: 0 ━━━━━━━━ 1 KM
        ½ MILE

Start at: Ⓐ

- 24 -

Walk 10

Distance: 5 km (3½m) 1-1½ hrs
Start Point: Thorington Street (GR 011353)
Route: Stour Valley Path
Pubs: The Rose, Thorington Street
Car Park: Small lay-by next to 'phone box in Thorington Street.

A: Go along the B1068 towards Higham and Stratford St Mary. *Take care along here - it's a 'B' road, although quite narrow. Some motorists seem to be prejudiced against pedestrians* About 500m after leaving the village, just after passing Nether Hall on the right, turn left on a track, signed Stour Valley Path. In about 1km the track becomes a lane with trees on both sides. Stay in this pleasant shady lane for about 600m to reach the corner of a metalled lane with a farm to your left. Go straight on along the road for about 350m to reach a signed track to the left.

B: Turn left, following signs for the Stour Valley path. In about 300m, just after passing Bobwrights Farm, turn right across the field on a signed track, still following the Stour Valley path. Stay on this path, crossing a metalled road in about 400m, to reach a wide, unsurfaced track in about another 200m.

C: Turn right up the track, leaving the Stour Valley path, to reach a road in about 400m. At the road, immediately turn left down a pleasant hedged lane. Near the bottom, when you're level with a red brick house, bear right to continue down to the river Box.

D: After crossing the river, turn left, keeping to the river bank. In about 500m watch for a waymark taking you right for a few steps, then on again across the open field. *(NB At the time of writing, there is a diversion application to divert the path along the edge of the river, then up the next field edge to reach the same point - please observe any FP signs to this effect).* The path continues along the field edge straight ahead. Keep along the field edge to reach a gap on the left in about 400m. Go through the gap and continue on the other side of the hedge for about 100m to reach the road on a bend.

E: Turn right on the road to reach the B1068 near the Rose Inn in about 300m.

Map 11

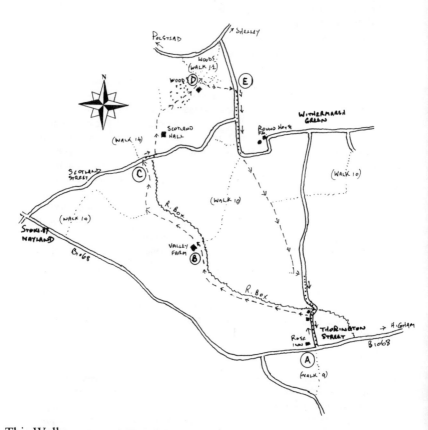

This Walk: → – – → ▭▭▭▭▭ – → → – – →
Roads: ═══════════════
Other Paths/Walks: ·····················
Scale: |—————————————| 1 KM
⅟₂ MILE

Start at: Ⓐ

- 26 -

Walk 11

Distance: 6km (4m) 1½-2 hrs
Start Point: Thorington Street (GR 011353)
Route: Thorington Street Circular
Pubs: The Rose Inn, Thorington Street
Car Park: Small lay-by next to 'phone box in Thorington Street.

A: Walk up the by-road opposite the 'phone box as far as the right hand bend then turn left on the signed path into the field. In about 100m go through the obvious gap on the left to continue along on the other side of the hedge. When you reach the open field in 500m, follow waymark signs taking you to the bank of the River Box, then continue along the river.

B: After passing Valley Farm on the left in 500m, continue straight on along the track - where the track bends left, cross the stile and go straight on along the waymarked field edge. Continue along field edges for about 800m, ignoring the Stour Valley Path signed across the field in about 500m You should emerge on a road almost opposite Scotland Place.

C: Turn right on the road and walk along to a signed footpath on the left in 150m. Cross the stile and go across the field following the direction of several yellow arrows. About 150m after passing Scotland Hall up to your right, cross a stile on the right with 2 separate footpaths signed. Take the path heading uphill towards the woods. Cross the next stile and continue on the clear track uphill through the woods. At the top you'll enter a clearing and pass farm buildings on the right. Go straight on to enter woods again for only a few steps.

D: Turn right on the woodland ride just inside the wood. In about 50m go half left to cross a stile onto a wide track along the edge of the wood. Turn left and walk along to the road.

E: At the road, turn right, soon passing a right hand turn to Colchester and Stoke. Ignore the footpath on the right 250m after this, and continue for 100m to the next left hand bend to find 2 bridleways. Take the second of these, more or less straight ahead and follow it downhill to a T-junction in about 1km. At the T-junction turn briefly left, then right on the road, bringing you back to your start point in about 500m.

Map 12

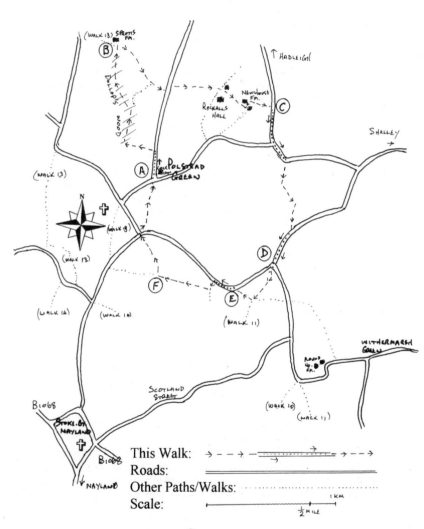

This Walk: → - - → ——→—— → + - →
Roads: ══════════
Other Paths/Walks: ·····················
Scale: |————————————| 1 KM
                ½ MILE

Start at: Ⓐ

- 28 -

Walk 12

Distance: 6½km (4m) 1½-2 hrs
Start Point: Polstead Green (GR 993383)
Route: Polstead Circular
Pubs: The Cock Inn, Polstead Green
Car Park: *Parking is difficult in Polstead but if you're using the pub, it may be possible to use their car park - check with the landlord on 01206-263150 first.*

A: Leave Polstead Green by the road to the left of the Cock Inn. In 300m, after passing the playing field, turn left through a gateway. Walk down to the wood (Dollop's Wood). About 50m into the wood, turn right following painted yellow arrows. In 300m, where arrows indicate a fork, keep left. In about another 400m you'll reach a T-junction with a wide track near a farm.

B: Turn right at the T-junction. Shortly afterwards, bear right on a grassy track. This soon becomes a field edge. Cross the stile in the next corner and go along the lane to reach a road. At the road, turn left for 50m, then turn right on a signed track. Go straight on past the thatched cottage, and in about another 250m turn left between a large house and farm buildings, then stay on the concrete farm road, reaching a narrow public road in about 150m.

C: Turn right on the road. In about 250m, go straight on past a right hand turn, and in another 150m, where the road bends sharp left, go straight on along a track. In about 150m, just before the track bends left, turn left into a leafy lane. Stay in this pleasant lane, bringing you out on a narrow road in about 400m. Turn right on the road and walk along for 300m to reach a junction.

D: At the junction cross the road to a footpath signed into the wood straight ahead. *(Go down the left side of the wood for a few steps to find the start of the path)* Follow yellow arrows through the wood for 300m to reach a woodland ride. Go straight across the ride, then immediately turn right on a signed path, again following yellow arrows. Follow these to reach a road in about 250m.

E: Turn left on the road. In about 150m, turn left on a signed path for a few steps, then go right through a metal kissing gate on another signed path. At a metalled private road in about 200m, turn right briefly then left again to continue on along the flank of the hill. In about 300m you'll reach a stile.

F: After crossing the stile, turn right, parallel to the field edge, then more or less straight on as the path drops steeply down to a stile onto the road. Go up the road opposite for a few steps, to reach a path on your right signed Polstead Green. Follow this clear path uphill to emerge near the Cock Inn.

Map 13

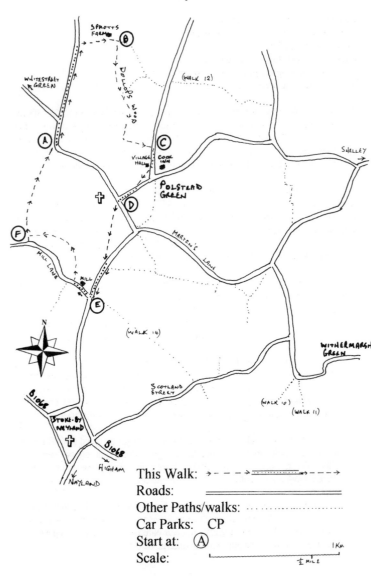

This Walk: → - - - → ══════ → - - →
Roads: ══════════
Other Paths/walks: ....
Car Parks: CP
Start at: Ⓐ
Scale: |⊢——————————⊣ 1 Km
          ⊢——————⊣ ½ Mile

- 30 -

Walk 13

Distance: 5½km (3½m) 1-1½ hrs
Start Point: Polstead (GR 985385)
Route: Polstead Circular
Pubs: The Cock Inn, Polstead Green
Car Park: *Approaching from Stoke-by-Nayland, go past the turn to Polstead Green, then past the drive to Polstead Church, and in 700m park where the road bends sharp right..*

A: Leave the car and continue up the road. Go straight past the left turn to Whitestreet Green in 150m and keep on to pass under the power lines. 200m further on, where the road bends right and left, turn right on a signed footpath to Sprotts Farm. Keep straight on between buildings to reach a signed path along a wooded valley to the right.

B: Turn right and follow this pleasant woodland path. checking your route by occasional painted yellow arrows. In about 800m watch out for an arrow up to the left taking you out of the wood. After leaving the wood, keep more or less straight on to reach a road.

C: Turn right on the road to reach Polstead Green next to the Cock Inn in 300m. Just after the village hall, go slightly right down a signposted path to cut the corner and reach the road in about 150m. Continue down the hill to the bottom.

D: At the T-junction at the bottom go straight across onto the signed footpath opposite. After a short climb up the grassy slope you'll see Polstead Church to your right. Stoke-by-Nayland church is about 2km straight ahead. Aim for this to reach the corner of a road in 400m. Go straight on along the road for about 400m to reach Mill Lane on the right.

E: Turn right into Mill Lane. About 50m after passing Polstead Mill turn right on a signed path. After crossing a stile in about 200m, the path gradually bears left, and you'll soon be walking along a field edge with a stream on your right. Continue along the field edge for about 300m to reach a gate into a lane.

F: Turn right in the lane, almost immediately crossing the stream and continue up the lane to reach your car in about 800m.

Map 14

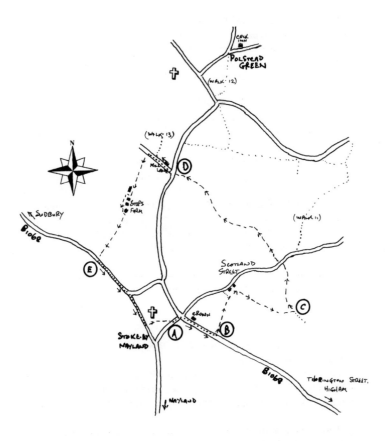

COW INN

POLSTEAD GREEN

(WALK 12)

(WALK 13)

MILL LANE

D

STEPS FARM

↑ SUDBURY

B1068

(WALK 11)

SCOTLAND STREET

E

A

B

CROWN

C

STOKE BY NAYLAND

B1068

THORINGTON STREET, HIGHAM

↓ NAYLAND

This Walk: → - - → ⟶⋯⋯⋯⋯⟶ → - - → ⟶
Roads: ══════
Other Paths/walks: ⋯⋯⋯⋯⋯⋯⋯⋯⋯⋯⋯⋯⋯⋯
Car Parks: CP
Start at: A
Scale: ⊢————————┤ 1 KM
                    ½ MILE

Walk 14

Distance: 5½km (3½m) 1-1½ hrs
Start Point: Stoke-by-Nayland (GR 987363)
Route: Scotland Street, Polstead Mill, Stoke-by-Nayland Church
Pubs: The Angel Inn, The Black Horse, The Crown
Car Park: Park in the side road between the Angel and the Church.

A: Go back up to the B1068, and turn right past the Crown, towards Higham. Walk along for about 350m, using the verge where possible, to reach a signed footpath to the left.

B: Turn left along the field-edge footpath. In about 400m, continue along the field edge past the backs of cottages. The field edge soon swings right. Follow it for about another 400m to reach an open field. Here go slightly left across the field to reach the far field edge.

C: On the other side of the field, turn **left** and follow the field edge path to reach the road at Scotland Street. Here go slightly left onto the footpath almost opposite.   You'll soon reach an open field. Keep to the right hand field edge for about 100m, then go through an obvious gap to continue on the good track on the other side. Stay on this path along the field edge to reach the road at Polstead, almost opposite Mill Lane.

D: Go along Mill Lane, and about 150m after passing Polstead Mill, turn left on a signed path with the hedge on your right. In about 400m, just after a low building on the right, turn right and then left onto a field edge path, to bypass the other farm buildings, then follow signs to continue up the hill to reach the outskirts of Stoke-by-Nayland.

E: When you reach the road at the top, turn left and head straight for the church.   Just after passing the church, turn left on the signed footpath taking you back to your car.

Map 15

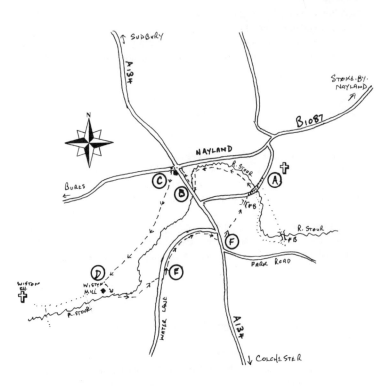

This Walk:
Roads:
Other Paths/walks:
Car Parks: CP
Start at: (A)
Scale:

1 KM

½ MILE

Walk 15

Distance: 5km (3m)   1 - 1½ hrs
Start Point: Nayland (GR 974343)
Route: Stour Valley Path, Wiston Mill
Pubs: The Anchor
Car Park: Park by the War Memorial near the church.

A: Continue down the road past the War Memorial. After crossing the bridge, turn immediately right down the steps, and along the river bank. Follow this along to reach the A134, in about 1km.

B: Turn right along the wide greensward of the A134, and walk along to the cross-roads (Nag's Corner). Cross the road with care, and go up the road opposite for a short distance.

C: A few steps along the road turn left over a stile onto the Stour Valley Path. Follow this well signed path along field edges for about 1km as far as Wiston Mill.

D: By Wiston Mill, turn left on the signed path to cross the mill stream over a wooden bridge. Go straight on to the fence, then bear left along the fence to reach a footbridge over the Stour in about 150m. Immediately after crossing the bridge, turn left along the bank for about 100m. Just after crossing a rough bridge by a pond, follow yellow arrows to take you out onto the road. (Water Lane).

E: Turn left along the lane and follow it along to the main road. (The field edge on the right hand side of the lane is a public footpath all the way to the main road, but you may prefer walking on the road.)

F: When you reach the main road, cross this very fast stretch of the A134 with care. At the footpath sign almost opposite, cross the field directly towards the wooden hump-backed bridge about 300m distant. If the path is not clear, follow the direction of the signpost. (The field edge is not a right of way.)

G: At the other side, cross the bridge and turn right up the road past the Anchor to return to your car.

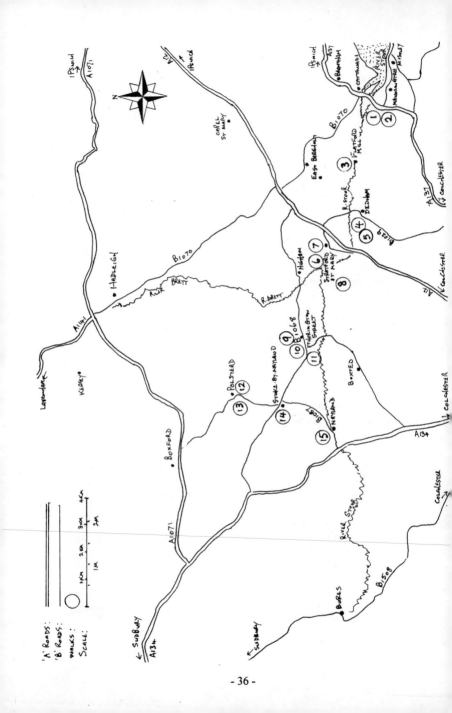